C000255953

1 MONTH OF FREE READING

at

www.ForgottenBooks.com

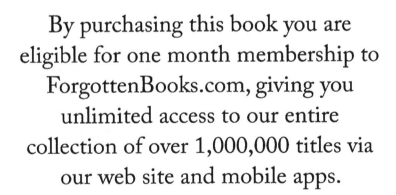

By purchasing this book you are eligible for one month membership to ForgottenBooks.com, giving you unlimited access to our entire collection of over 1,000,000 titles via our web site and mobile apps.

To claim your free month visit:

www.forgottenbooks.com/free989302

ISBN 978-0-332-68428-4
PIBN 10989302

OF

A COMMITTEE

Appointed by Resolution

Adopted at the Annual Meeting, October, 1887,

and continued in 1888, to October, 1889.

◁ÆZTEC CLUB OF 1847▷

Founded in the City of Mexico, A. D. 1847.

—— PUBLISHED IN 1890.——

WASHINGTON, D. C. :

JUDD & DETWEILER, PRINTERS.

1890.

Obv.   Aztec Club of 1847.   Rev.

California Veterans,
Mexican War.

National Association
Mexican War Veterans.

G. A. R. First Badge, 1866–1869.

AZTEC CLUB OF 1847.

Report of a Committee of THE AZTEC CLUB appointed at the meeting held in the city of New York, October 13, 1887, in accordance with the following resolution:

"*Resolved,* That a committee, consisting of the President, General Hagner, and General Palmer, be appointed to revise the list of members, and give to each his proper title."

Upon receipt of the above notice, meetings were held in the city of Washington to consider the form of report most suitable to meet the expressed wishes of the members, and to be of continued usefulness in the future existence of the Club.

Our records show that at the time of the withdrawal of our Army from Mexico the Aztec Club consisted of 160 members and 2 honorary members; that at a meeting in May, 1848, it was determined that no satisfactory plan could be then proposed for continuing the existence of the Club after returning home; but, "desiring to preserve some lasting memorial of the pleasure and advantages derived from this institution that may serve for all time as an additional bond of friendship and brotherhood among its members," it was

"*Resolved,* That the organization of the Club shall continue with its present officers for a period of five years from the 14th September, 1847."

In 1852 an election of new officers was made accordingly, but no regular meeting of the Club took place until September, 1867, when officers were elected, a place and day for the next annual meeting named, a list of the original members ordered to be printed and distributed, and a commemoration badge to be designed for transmission to living members and to the families of those deceased.

The action taken at this meeting was submitted to the survivors of the Aztec Club of 1847, and confirmed by the votes returned to the secretary.

At future regular meetings resolutions have been adopted, in accordance with Article XII of the Constitution of 1847, as follows:

In 1871 it was decided to admit to membership officers who may apply, having served in any part of Mexico during the war, after nomination and election by the Club.

In 1882 it was decided that officers killed in battle or who died of wounds in Mexico before the formation of the Club might, upon application of a son or nearest blood relative, be admitted to the roll of membership, to be represented by the son or nearest blood relative, after his nomination and election by the Club.

In 1887 it was decided that officers now deceased who served in Mexico during the war, never members of the Club but eligible to membership if living, may be admitted to the roll of membership, each to be represented by his nearest blood relative, when duly elected by the Club, upon the written application of such blood relative, approved by two members, to whom he is known.

Under these several decisions the whole number of members now enrolled—officers who personally served in Mexico during the war with that country—is as follows:

By the original list admitted in the City of Mexico 160
Under resolution of 1871, upon personal application 50
Under resolution of 1883 (killed in battle), application by representative 4
Under resolution of 1887, application by representative 9
                                                                   ———
        Total to October, 1889 223

In consideration of the foregoing, showing the expressed desire of the original Club in May, 1848, " to preserve for all time some lasting memorial that may serve as an additional bond of friendship and brotherhood among its members;" the continuance of the AZTEC CLUB OF 1847 in "perpetuity," as expressed in the constitution of 1887 and again in the revised constitution of 1888, the committee deem it decided that the Club should be known—

1st. As the "Aztec Club of 1847."

2d. That it is to be continued in "perpetuity."

3d. That the basis of "membership" is *personal service in some part of Mexico, "as an officer, during the war with that country."*

Therefore, the committee propose that the lists of members, as *revised*, should embrace the names of—

1st. All members admitted in Mexico in 1848.

2d. All admitted and who may be admitted under resolution of 1871.

3d. All admitted and who may be admitted under resolution of 1883.

4th. All admitted and who may be admitted under resolution of 1887.

This *"Roll of Primary Members"* should be arranged in numerical series, alphabetically (as far as convenient) in the order of admittance, to remain undisturbed *except* by additions, or by dismissal for cause.

On List No. 1 members' names will be entered in columns, using different type to show those *living, dead*, and *in service;* the number assigned to each name to remain unaltered, with the *rank and corps of each while serving in Mexico*, and the *brevets* bestowed for *Mexican service.*

On List No. 2 the primary members' names will be given, with the number belonging to each, as in List No. 1, and the recognized professional or military titles acquired since the

Mexican war will be affixed to each. The name and the degree of relationship of the successor or associate of living members and of the representatives of deceased members shall be entered on the line of the name, with the date of election of the representative.

List No. 3 should be·published from time to time as may be directed, giving the numbers and names of the primary members, and in ·line therewith the name of each blood relative who may then be the representative of the primary member and an active member of the Club at the date of publication.

———

WASHINGTON, *October*, 1888·.

The committee presented the above report at the meeting held at Chamberlin's, October, 1888, asking that, if acccepted by the Club, it should be also considered as a proposition made at this meeting to change the constitution of 1887 to conform thereto.

It was then resolved that the report of General Hagner be accepted as a proposition made at this meeting to change the Constitution, and that the Committee on the Revised Lists be continued.

———

MEETING AT WORMLEY'S,
WASHINGTON, *October* 16, 1889.

The Committee on the Revised Lists respectfully report the accompanying modifications of the Constitution in accordance with the notice accepted at the last meeting.

The Constitution as proposed was then read, and, having been altered by adding the words "Navy and Marine Corps" after the word "Army," in the second line of Article II, on membership, so as to read " as an officer of the Army, Navy, or Marine Corps," the vote upon the adoption of the Constitution as altered was taken, and it was agreed to.

The Committee on the Revised Lists, continued from the meeting of 1888, then presented its report upon the lists of members proposed to be published with the new Constitution.

The report was adopted, and it was ordered that 200 copies of this report, including the amended Constitution, be printed for distribution.

Upon motion of General Hagner, General W. W. H. Davis was added to the Committee on Printing.

WASHINGTON, 1890.

CONSTITUTION OF THE AZTEC CLUB OF 1847.

Revised and Adopted October 16th, 1889.

ARTICLE I.—*Object.*

This Association, formed and founded in the City of Mexico, in the year 1847, by officers of the United States Army, shall be continued in perpetuity as "The Aztec Club of 1847," with a view to cherish the memories and keep alive the traditions that cluster about the names of those officers who took part in the Mexican War of 1846, '47, and '48·

Officers of the U. S. Navy and Marine Corps who served in Mexico during the War are equally eligible with Army officers.

ARTICLE II.—*Membership.*

The basis of Primary Membership being personal service as an officer of the Army, Navy, or Marine Corps in some part of Mexico during the war with that country in 1846, '47, and '48, the Roll of Members to be "continued in perpetuity" under this Constitution shall consist :

First. Of those officers who inaugurated the Aztec Club in the City of Mexico on the 13th of October 1847, numbering 160 members, and the two honorary members named in Articles I and IV of the Constitution published in March, 1848 ; and

Second. Of those officers who by resolution of 1871 became eligible to membership since that date, having served in some part of Mexico during the war with that country, and who have been or may hereafter be duly elected members. The names of members admitted upon personal application will be enrolled as Primary Members on a list (Number *One*) to be arranged permanently, in numerical series, in the order of date of admittance—not to be altered except by future *additions* or by *dismissals for cause.*

Third. To extend to the memory of comrades *killed in battle* in Mexico or who died of wounds received in Mexico prior to the formation of our Club, all the honorable distinction pertaining to membership in the Club, it was resolved in 1883 that upon application by the eldest son or nearest lineal descendant of the officer so killed such son or lineal descendant may be eligible to membership as representing his dead relative. When such representative has been duly elected and qualified, the name of the dead officer and the battle where he was killed should be entered on List Number *One*, in a separate group with his representative, in the order of election.

Fourth. As provided in 1887, the son or nearest blood relative of any deceased officer who never himself applied for membership (though eligible thereto because of personal service in Mexico during the war) may make written application for admission as the representative of his father or blood relative, upon nomination by two members to whom he is known. If elected and qualified the name of such dead officer shall also be enrolled on List Number *One*, in the same numerical series, in a separate group, and in the order of the date of admittance of the lineal descendant.

FUTURE ACTIVE MEMBERSHIP.

Fifth. To provide for the continuance of the Club in conformity with the resolution of September, 1874, each Primary Member admitted upon personal application may nominate as his successor his son or a blood relative, who during the life of the Primary shall be known as an Associate Member, and entitled to all the privileges of the Club except that of voting, and upon the death of the Primary shall be entitled as his representative to full membership. Should a Primary die without having named his successor, his son (*first*) or nearest blood relative (*next*) may, on written application, be nominated as his representative by two members to whom he is known; but no one proposed for an Associate Member or as the representative of a deceased member shall be voted for until the Examining Committee shall report him eligible and qualified to join the Club. If minors are proposed their names will be retained for future action until they attain majority.

Election of members will take place only at the regular meetings of the Club. At least thirteen affirmative votes (in *person* or *by letter*) shall be required to admit the applicant, while two negative votes will reject him.

A Representative Member may present a blood relative of the Primary Member he represents, as his own associate, and, if elected, he will be entitled to the privileges of an Associate Member, and upon the death of the representative may himself become a Representative Member, and in like manner nominate as his associate the nearest living blood relative of the dead Primary Member, if there be one qualified to become an acceptable representative of said Primary. When no such lineal descendant of the Primary Member exists the succession for such member of the Aztec Club will cease.

The initation fees shall be payable to the Treasurer of the Club upon each election as follows :

For New Members or their Representative Members . $25 00
For Associate Members 5 00

Should an elected applicant neglect for ten (10) months after election to send his acceptance and pay the prescribed fee, his name shall be reported to the Club by the Treasurer for its action at the next regular meeting, and unless a good reason for such neglect is presented his name shall be dropped.

ARTICLE III.—*Insignia of Membership.*

Each member shall be entitled to receive a medal struck from the dies belonging to the club, and also a diploma, from the plate in its possession. These medals and diplomas are to descend to the duly elected representatives of the deceased members. The medals are to be worn at all regular meetings.

The dies for the medal and the plate for the diploma shall be retained in the custody of the Treasurer, and shall be used only for multiplying copies in compliance with the vote of the Club.

A tri-colored button authorized by the Club may be furnished at cost to each member and associate member.

ARTICLE IV.—*Officers.*

1. The officers of the Club shall be a President and a Vice-President, Treasurer and a Vice-Treasurer, a Secretary, and an Assistant Secretary.

2. The Vice-President shall be elected annually, and at the end of his term of service shall become the President of the Club for the next year.

3. In the case of death or resignation of the President or Treasurer, the Vice-President, or Vice-Treasurer, shall immediately succeed to the respective chief office without other election, and at the next regular meeting all vacant offices shall be filled.

4. Should the office of Secretary become vacant the Assistant Secretary shall take charge of the records until the position is filled by the election of a Secretary.

5. The Secretary may appoint his Assistant from either the members or the associate members of the Club. All other officers shall be chosen by ballot.

ARTICLE V.—*Duties of the Treasurer.*

The Treasurer shall be held responsible for the funds of the Club, shall disburse them under its direction, and report yearly the Club's financial condition.

ARTICLE VI.—*Duties of the Secretary.*

The Secretary shall keep a record of the Club's proceedings, conduct its correspondence, notify members at least one month in advance of its regular and special meetings, keep and affix its seal, preserve its archives, and perform such other duties appropriate to the office of Secretary as the Executive Committee may direct.

ARTICLE VII.—*Executive Committee.*

There shall be a permanent Executive Committee of the Club, to consist of its President and Vice-President, Treasurer and Secretary, and three other members to be appointed and removable by the President, to act for the Club in the intervals between its regular meetings. Three of the Executive Committee designated by the President shall constitute a sub-committee, to examine and report to the Club at its regular meetings upon qualifications of applicants for admission.

ARTICLE VIII.—*Quorum.*

Business may be transacted at any duly appointed meeting of the Club, provided the number of members present shall not be less shan *eleven* (11), and that not less than *nine* (9) affirmative votes be given to carry any measure proposed.

ARTICLE IX.—*Suspension of Members.*

The President of the Club shall take notice of any irregularities that may disturb the harmony of its social or business meetings. Should his admonitions be unheeded he may suspend the offending member from the privileges of the Club, until his action shall be reversed by a majority vote of its members at an annual meeting.

ARTICLE X.—*Alterations.*

Any proposition to alter this Constitution must be made at a regular meeting of the Club, action thereon to be taken at the next regular meeting.

BY-LAWS.

—————

I.—*Order of Business.*

1. Meeting called to order.
2. Roll-call.
3. Minutes of the previous meeting read and disposed of.
4. Report of Secretary.
5. Report of Treasurer.
6. Report of committees.
7. Unfinished business.
8. Candidates for election to membership considered.
9. Election of officers.
10. New business considered.
11. Time and place of next meeting decided.
12. Adjournment.

II.—*Guests.*

Guests not exceeding five in number may be admitted to the annual banquets of the Club by special invitation of the Executive Committee. The expense incurred on account of a guest must be borne by the member at whose instance he is invited.

III.—*Archives.*

Each member is requested to send to the Secretary his photograph, bearing his autograph, and also a short biographical sketch of himself. These will be preserved among the archives of the Club in the hands of the Secretary.

IV.—*Post-Office Addresses.*

Members must keep the Secretary informed of their post-office address.

SEAL OF THE ÆZTEC CLUB,

ADOPTED IN 1849.

LIST NO. 1.

NAMES OF THE ORIGINAL MEMBERS

OF THE

AZTEC CLUB OF 1847,

INCLUDING

Those since admitted, who served in Mexico during the War.

CORRECTED TO JANUARY, 1890.

— Those now in service.   Italics — Living.   Roman — Deceased.

No. of name.	Rank and names.	Corps.	Brevets for service in Mexico.
1847–8			
1	Bvt. Maj. J. J. Abercrombie --	1st Infantry ---------	Lieutenant Col.
2	Capt. T. L. Alexander --- ----	6th Infantry --------	Major.
3	Capt. Robert Allen ----- ----	Assistant Q. M. ------	Major.
4	*Lt. S. S. Anderson* ----------	2d Artillery----- ----	Capt. and major.
5	Lt. B. H. Arthur ------------	1st Infantry.	
6	Capt. Electus Backus --- ---	1st Infantry ---------	Major.
7	Maj. Henry Bainbridge------	7th Infantry ----- ---	Lieutenant Col.
8	Capt. J. G. Barnard---------	Engineers ------- ---	Major.
9	Capt. M. J. Barnard --------	Voltigeurs.	
10	Lt. Jenks Beaman ----------	4th Infantry.	
11	*Lt. P. G. T. Beauregard* ----	Engineers ----------	Capt. and major.
12	2d Lt. Barnard E. Bee -------	3d Infantry ----------	1st Lt. and Capt.
13	Lt. Col. Francis S. Belton----	3d Artillery----------	Colonel.
14	Capt. Charles J. Biddle ------	Voltigeurs -----------	Major.
15	Lt. William B. Blair---------	2d Artillery ---------	Captain.
16	Capt. George A. H. Blake----	2d Dragoons ---------	Major.
17	*Capt. James D. Blanding* ----	S. C. Vols., Palmetto.	
18	Capt. William Blanding - ---	S. C. Vols., Palmetto.	
19	*Col. Milledge L. Bonham* ---	12th Infantry.	
20	Lt. Andrew W. Bowman-----	3d Infantry ----------	Captain.
21	*Lt. John M. Brannan* ------	1st Artillery----------	Captain.
22	*Capt. Horace Brooks* -------	2d Artillery----------	Maj. and Lt. Col.
23	Lt. William T. H. Brooks----	3d Infantry ------ ---	Capt. and major.
24	Lt. Hachaliah Brown -------	3d Artillery----------	Captain.
25	Maj. Robert C. Buchanan----	4th Infantry ---------	Maj. and Lt. Col.
26	Brig. Gen. Geo. Cadwalader--	U. S. Army ---------	Major general.
27	Capt. Albemarle Cady -------	6th Infantry ---------	Major.
28	*Maj. G. A. Caldwell* --- ----	Voltigeurs.	
29	Lt. Robert C. Caldwell-------	Marine Corps.	
30	*Lt. George W. Carr* ----- ---	Voltigeurs.	
31	Capt. Daniel T. Chandler ---	3d Infantry ----------	Maj. and Lt. Col.
32	*Maj. P. St. George Cooke*---	2d Dragoons ---------	Lieutenant Col.
33	*Lt. Henry Coppée* ----------	1st Artillery----------	Captain.
34	Capt. Louis S. Craig -------	3d Infantry ---------	Maj. and Lt. Col.

(13)

No. of name.	Rank and names.	Corps.	Brevets for service in Mexico.
1847-8			
35	Surg. Presly H. Craig	Medical Staff.	
36	Lt. Alexander H. Cross	Voltigeurs.	
37	Capt. Joseph Daniels	Assistant Q. M., Vols.	
38	Maj. J. Y. Dashiell	Pay Dept., Vols.	
39	Capt. George Deas	Asst. Adjt. Gen.	Major.
40	Asst. Surg. D. C. DeLeon	Medical Staff.	
41	Lt. F. J. Denman	1st Infantry.	
42	Bvt. Maj. James Duncan	2d Artillery	Lt. Col. and Col.
43	Lt. Richard S. Ewell	1st Dragoons	Captain.
44	Lt. Col. Thos. T. Fauntleroy	2d Dragoons.	
45	Capt. Edward H. Fitzgerald	9th Infantry.	
46	2d Lt. Robert C. Forsyth	Voltigeurs	1st lieutenant.
47	Lt. William H. French	1st Artillery	Capt. and major.
48	*2d Lt. Daniel M. Frost*	Mounted Rifles	1st lieutenant.
49	Maj. A. W. Gaines	Pay Dept., Vols.	
50	Maj. Patrick H. Galt	2d Artillery	Lieutenant Col.
51	Lt. John W. T. Gardiner	1st Dragoons.	
52	*Capt. Richard C. Gatlin*	7th Infantry	Major.
53	2d Lt. Alfred Gibbs	Mounted Rifles	1st Lt. and Capt.
54	*Lt. C. C. Gilbert*	1st Infantry.	
55	Lt. Col. Adley H. Gladden	S. C. Vols., Palmetto.	
56	Lt. John H. Gore	4th Infantry	Capt. and major.
57	Lt. Henry D. Grafton	1st Artillery	Captain.
58	Lt. Ulysses S. Grant	4th Infantry	Captain.
59	Capt. John B. Grayson	Commissary Dept.	Maj. and Lt. Col.
60	Maj. Maxy Gregg	12th Infantry.	
61	*Lt. Peter V. Hagner*	Ordnance	Capt. and major.
62	Capt. O. P. Hamilton	12th Infantry.	
63	*2d Lt. Schuyler Hamilton*	1st Infantry	1st Lt. and Capt.
64	Lt. Richard P. Hammond	3d Artillery	Capt. and major.
65	*2d Lt. Ed. L. F. Hardcastle*	Top. Engineers	1st Lt. and Capt.
66	Capt. William J. Hardee	2d Dragoons	Maj. and Lt. Col.
67	Surg. Benjamin F. Harney	Medical Staff.	
68	Col. William S. Harney	2d Dragoons	Brigadier Gen.
69	*2d Lt. John P. Hatch*	Mounted Rifles	1st Lt. and Capt.
70	Capt. John S. Hatheway	1st Artillery	Major.
71	Lt. Col. Paul O. Hébert	14th Infantry	Colonel.
72	Capt. W. S. Henry	3d Infantry	Major.
73	Capt. William Hoffmann	6th Infantry	Maj. and Lt. Col.
74	2d Lt. E. B. Holloway	8th Infantry	1st lieutenant.
75	Capt. Joseph Hooker	Asst. Adjt. Gen.	Maj. and Lt. Col.
76	Capt. John Eager Howard	Voltigeurs.	
77	Capt. Benjamin Huger	Ordnance	Maj. and Lt. Col.
78	Capt. James R. Irwin	Assistant Q. M.	
79	*Lt. Col. Joseph E. Johnston*	Voltigeurs	Lt. Col. and Col.
80	Lt. Llewellyn Jones	Mounted Rifles.	
81	Capt. Philip Kearny	1st Dragoons	Major.
82	Maj. Edmund Kirby	Pay Department	Lt. Col. and Col.
83	Asst. Surg. C. H. Laub	Medical Staff	Lieutenant Col.
84	2d Lt. George W. Lay	6th Infantry	1st Lt. and Capt.

No. of name.	Rank and names.	Corps.	Brevets for service in Mexico.
1847–8			
85	Capt. Robert E. Lee---------	Engineers -----------	Maj., Lt. Col., &
86	Lt. Mansfield Lovell----------	4th Artillery---------	Captain. [Col.
87	Capt. Roland A. Luther -----	2d Artillery.	
88	2d Lt. George B. McClellan--	Engineers -----------.	1st Lt. and Capt.
89	Lt. Philip W. McDonald-----	2d Dragoons ---------	Capt. and major.
90	*Capt. Samuel McGowan*-----	Assistant Q. M., Vols.	
91	*Capt. William W. Mackall*--	Asst. Adjt. Gen.-------	Major.
92	*Capt. Justus McKinstry* -----	Assistant Q. M. ------	Major.
93	2d Lt. George McLane-------	Mounted Rifles ------	1st Lt. and Capt.
94	Capt. John B. Magruder -----	1st Artillery----------	Maj. and Lt. Col.
95	Lt. James R. May ----------	Voltigeurs.	
96	2d Lt. Julian May ----------	Mounted Rifles ------	1st lieutenant.
97	Maj. Albert S. Miller--------	1st Infantry.	
98	*2d Lt. Robert M. Morris* - --	Mounted Rifles ------	1st Lt. and Capt.
99	Capt. Thompson Morris-------	2d Infantry ----------	Maj. and Lt. Col.
100	Lt. F. S. Mumford -----------	1st Infantry.	
101	Maj. John Munroe-----------	4th Artillery --------	Lt. Col. and Col.
102	Capt. Abraham C. Myers ----	Assistant Q. M. ------	Maj. and Lt. Col.
103	Lt. Anderson D. Nelson------	6th Infantry.	
104	Lt. W. I. Newton------------	2d Dragoons.	
105	Capt. W. A. Nichols- -------	2d Artillery----------	Capt. and major.
106	Capt. Theodore O'Hara------	A. Q. M. Volunteers--	Major.
107	Capt. Francis N. Page-------	Asst. Adjt. General---	Major.
108	*2d Lt. Innis N. Palmer* ----	Mounted Rifles -- ----	1st Lt. and Capt.
109	Maj. Genl. Robert Patterson-	Volunteer Service.	
110	Bvt. Capt. John C. Pemberton-	4th Artillery ----- ---	Capt. and major.
111	Brig. Genl. Franklin Pierce--	Volunteer Service.	
112	Maj. William H. Polk-------	3d Dragoons.	
113	Capt. Andrew Porter-------.	Mounted Rifles-------	Maj. and Lt. Col.
114	*Lt. Fitz John Porter*-------	4th Artillery ---------	Capt. and major.
115	Lt. Col. William Preston-----	4th Kentucky Vols.	
116	Maj. Genl. John A. Quitman-	U. S. Army ---------	Major general.
117	*Lt. George W. Rains*--------	4th Artillery ---------	Captain.
118	Surgeon Burton Randall-----	Medical Staff.	
119	2d Lt. Jesse L. Reno---------	Ordnance -----------	1st Lt. and Capt.
120	Lt. Thomas G. Rhett -------	Mounted Rifles-------	Captain.
121	Surg. Robert R. Ritchie------	Maj. & Surg. 12th Inf.	
122	Lt. Roswell S. Ripley-------	2d Artillery----------	Capt. and major.
123	2d Lt. Francis S. K. Russell--	Mounted Rifles-------	1st lieutenant.
124	Capt. Henry L. Scott -------	A. A. Adjt. General--	Maj. and Lt. Col.
125	*Lt. Oliver L. Shepherd*----	3d Infantry ---------	Capt. and major.
126	2d Lt. Hamilton L. Shields---	3d Artillery ---------	1st Lt. and Capt.
127	Capt. Henry H. Sibley------	2d Dragoons -----,---	Major.
128	Asst. Surg. James Simons-- --	Medical Staff.	[Col.
129	Capt. Charles F. Smith ------	2d Artillery----------	Maj.,Lt. Col., and
130	*2d Lt. Gustavus W. Smith*---	Engineers -----------	1st Lt. and Capt.
131	2d Lt. Martin L. Smith ------	Top. Engineers ------	1st lieutenant.
132	Bvt. Brig. Genl. P. F. Smith-	Col. Mounted Rifles--	Brig. general and
133	Lt. William Steele ----------	2d Dragoons ---------	Capt. [Maj. Gen.
134	Capt. Edward J. Steptoe -----	3d Artillery ----- ----	Maj. and Lt. Col.

No. of name.	Rank and names.	Corps.	Brevets for service in Mexico.
1847-8			
135	Maj. Adam D. Steuart -------	Pay Department ------	Lieut. colonel.
136	2d Lt. Charles P. Stone ------	Ordnance -----------	1st Lt. and Capt.
137	2d Lt. James Stuart----------	Mounted Rifles.	1st Lt. and Capt.
138	Lt. George Sykes-----------	3d Infantry ---------	Captain.
139	Lt. Francis J. Thomas--------	3d Artillery.	
140	Capt. Philip R. Thompson----	1st Dragoons---- ----	Major.
141	Lt. Herman Thorn ----------	3d Dragoons.	
142	Lt. James Tilton-------------	Voltigeurs.	
143	Capt. John B. S. Todd --------	6th Infantry.	
144	*2d Lt. Zealous B. Tower --	Engineers -----------	1st Lt. Capt. and
145	Surg. Charles S. Tripler -----	Medical Staff.	[Maj.
146	Maj. William Turnbull ------	Top. Engineers ------	Lt. Col. and Col.
147	Brig. Genl. D. E. Twiggs ----	U. S. Army ---------	Major general.
148	Maj. Abraham Van Buren----	Pay Department ------	Lieut. colonel.
149	Lt. Earl Van Dorn ---------	7th Infantry---------	Capt. and major.
150	Maj. Richard D. A. Wade----	3d Artillery---------	Lieut. colonel.
151	2d Lt. Cadmus M. Wilcox---	7th Infantry---------	1st lieutenant.
152	*2d Lt. John D. Wilkins----	3d Infantry ---------	1st lieutenant.
153	Col. John S. Williams-------	4th Kentucky Vols.	
154	Lt. Thomas Williams---- ----	4th Artillery - -------	Capt. and major.
155	Col. Jones M. Withers-------	9th Infantry.	
156	Capt. George W. F. Wood----	A. Q. M.. ----------	Major.
157	2d Lt. Lafayette B. Wood----	8th Infantry - --- --	1st Lt. and Capt.
158	Lt. Francis Woodbridge-----	2d Artillery---------	Capt. and major.
159	Maj. Samuel Woods---------	15th Infantry ---- ----	Lieut. colonel.
160	Genl. William J. Worth------	U. S. Army ---------	Major general.

ART. I. Major General Winfield Scott, Commanding. { *Honorary Members*,
ART. IV. Rev. M. McCarty, Chaplain.   { *Constitution of 1847*.

Officers who Served in Mexico Admitted under Resolution of September, 1871.

No. of name.	Rank and names.	Corps.	Brevets for service in Mexico.
1873.			
161	Capt. Benjamin Alvord ------	4th Infantry ----- ----	Capt. and major.
162	Lt. William F. Barry -------	2d Artillery.	
163	2d Lt. Winfield S. Hancock--	6th Infantry---------	1st lieutenant.
164	*Capt. Henry L. Kendrick--	2d Artillery---------	Major.
165	*Capt. Henry Prince-------	4th Infantry --------	Capt. and major.
1879.			
166	2d Lt. Henry B. Clitz--------	3d Infantry ---------	1st lieutenant.
167	Capt. W. W. H. Davis------	Massachusetts Vols.	
168	*2d Lt. R. C. Drum --------	9th Infantry---------	1st lieutenant.
169	Lt. William H. Emory------	Top. Engineers ------	Capt. and major.
170	*2d Lt. De L. Floyd-Jones---	4th Infantry --------	1st lieutenant.
171	Lt. H. G. Gibson----------	3d Artillery.	
172	Capt. Silas Casey------------	2d Infantry ------ ----	Maj. and Lt. Col.

No. of name.	Rank and names.	Corps.	Brevets for service in Mexico.
1880.			
173	* *2d Lt. George W. Getty* ---	4th Artillery ----------	1st Lt. and Capt.
174	* *2d Lt. Thomas G. Pitcher* --	8th Infantry----------	1st lieutenant.
175	* *Lt. John C. Robinson* -------	5th Infantry.	
176	* *Lt. Stewart Van Vliet* ------	3d Artillery.	
177	* *Lt. Christopher C. Augur* --	4th Infantry.	
178	* *Maj. Benjamin W. Brice* --	Pay Department.	
179	Asst. Surg. C. H. Crane ---- ---	Medical Staff.	
1882.			
180	* *2d Lt. Gustavus A. DeRussy*	4th Artillery--------.---	1st lieutenant.
181	* *Capt. L. Pike Graham* ------	2d Dragoons----------	Major.
182	Lt. Henry J. Hunt-------- ---	2d Artillery ----------	Capt. and major.
183	*Lt. Andrew J. Lindsay* ------	Mounted Rifles.	
184	*Lt. James Longstreet* --------	8th Infantry----------	Capt. and major.
185	* *2d Lt. Joseph H. Potter* -----	7th Infantry----------	1st lieutenant.
186	2d Lt. Delos B. Sacket-------	2d Dragoons----------	1st lieutenant.
187	* *Lt. William T. Sherman*---	3d Artillery----- ----	Captain.
188	* *Lt. Col. T. L. Crittenden* --	3d Kentucky Vols.	
189	Maj. W. W. Loring------ ----	Mounted Rifles-------	Lt. Col. and Col.
190	* *2d Lt. James Oakes*--------	2d Dragoons- -------	1st Lt. and Capt.
1883.			
191	* *2d Lt. James B. Fry* . -----	1st Artillery.	
192	* *2d Lt. Rufus Ingalls*-------	1st Dragoons---- ----	1st lieutenant.
193	* *W. B. Lane*---- ----------	Mounted Rifles-------	2d lieutenant.
194	* *Capt. Daniel H. Rucker*----	1st Dragoons---------	Major.
195	Capt. C. F. Ruff------- ------	Mounted Rifles-------	Major.
1884.			
196	*Capt. Ed. L. Dana*----------	Pennsylvania Vols.	
197	2d Lt. Julian McAllister - ----	2d Artillery.	
1885.			
202	2d Lt. S. V. Niles------------	16th Infantry.	
1886.			
203	Capt. John H. King ---------	1st Infantry.	
204	* *2d Lt. George Thom*-------	Top. Engineers.	
205	2d Lt. Egbert L. Viele ------	1st Infantry.	
206	2d Lt. G. F. Hooper- ---- ---	15th Infantry.	
1887.			
207	Lt. Edmund Bradford -------	4th Artillery.	
208	*2d Lt. Wm. B. Franklin*-----	Top. Engineers ------	1st lieutenant.
209	* *Lt. Charles J. Sprague*- ----	9th Infantry----------	Captain.
210	* *2d Lt. O. B. Willcox*-------	4th Artillery.	
1888.			
217	2d Lt. F. T. Bryan----------	Top. Engineers ------	1st lieutenant.
218	2d Lt. D. N. Couch----------	4th Artillery ---------	1st lieutenant.
219	* *2d Lt. F. T. Dent*----------	5th Infantry -------.---	1st Lt. and Capt.
220	*2d Lt. Henry Heth* ----------	1st Infantry.	
221	2d Lt. Charles S. Merchant --	8th Infantry---------	1st Lt. and Capt.

Officers Killed in Mexico before the Formation of the Club, Entered on List of Members under Resolution of 1882—Represented, upon Application, by their Nearest Blood Relatives.

No. of name.	Rank and names.	Corps.	When and where killed.	Representative elected.
1884.				
198	Maj. Jacob Brown	7th Infantry	Fort Brown, 1846	His grandson, R. C. Van ?t, Army.
199	Lt. Chas. Hoskins	4th Infantry	Monterey, 1846	His son, J. D. C. Hoskins, Army.
200	Col. William R. McKee	2d Kentucky Vols.	Buena Vista, 1847	His son, G. W. Mc?, Army.
201	Capt. J. W. Anderson	2d Infantry	?o, 1847	His son, Ed. W. ?n, Esq.

Officers who Served in Mexico, never Members of the Club, who would, if Living, be Eligible thereto under Resolution of 1887—Represented by their Nearest Blood Relatives.

No. of name.	Rank and names.	Corps.	Brevets for service in Mexico.	Representatives elected.
1887.				
211	2d Lt. James M. Henry	2d Infantry	—	His son, James M. Henry, Esq.
212	2d Lt. F. B. Kaercher	Pennsylvania Vols.	—	His son, ?e B. Kaercher, Esq.
213	Capt. John McClellan	Top. Engineers	Maj. and Lt. Col.	His son, John McClellan, Army.
214	2d Lt. Geo. G. Meade	Top. Engineers	1st Lt.	His son, Geo. Meade, Esq.
215	Capt. E. S. Sibley	Ast. quartermaster.	Major	His son, F. T. Sibley, Esq.
216	Lt. J. F. Reynolds	4th Artillery	Capt. and major	His nephew, J. F. R. Landis, Army.
1888.				
222	Capt. J. P. J. O'Brien	4th Artillery	Major	His son, John F. O'Brien.
223	2d Lt. John M. Snyder	4th Kentucky Vols.	—	His son, Wm. Tayloe Snyder.

LIST NO. 2.

Names of Members of the Aztec Club of 1847, Designated by their Recognized Professional Titles, acquired since the Mexican War, with the Name and Date of Election of the Blood-Relative, as Associate or Representative.

No. of Names, List I.	Members' Names and Titles.	Blood-relative Elected.		Date.
		Relationship—Names.	Residence.	
1	General J. J. Abercrombie	*Son*, F. P. Abercrombie	Sunbury, Pa.	1884
2	Colonel T. L. Alexander.			
3	General Robert Allen.			
4	Colonel S. S. Anderson	*Son*, H. C. Anderson	Frankfort, Ky.	1886
5	Captain B. H. Arthur.			
6	Colonel Electus Backus.			
7	Colonel Henry Bainbridge.			
8	General J. G. Barnard	*Son*, A. P. Barnard	New York city, N. Y.	1879
9	Major M. J. Barnard.			
10	Lieutenant Jenks Beaman.			
11	General P. G. T. Beauregard	*Son*, H. T. Beauregard	New Orleans, La.	1879
12	General Barnard E. Bee.			
13	Colonel Francis S. Belton.			
14	Major Charles J. Biddle	*Son*, Charles Biddle	Philadelphia, Pa.	1880
15	Colonel William B. Blair.			
16	General George A. H. Blake.			
17	Colonel James D. Blanding	*Son*, William D. Blanding	Sumpter, S. C.	1886
18	Captain William Blanding	*Son*, Gordon Blanding	San Francisco, Cal.	1886
19	General Milledge L. Bonham	*Son*, M. L. Bonham	Columbia, S. C.	1886
20	Colonel Andrew W. Bowman.			
21	General John M. Brannan	*Nephew*, Dr. J. W. Brannan	New York city, N. Y.	1886
22	General Horace Brooks.			
23	General William T. H. Brooks.			
24	Captain Hachaliah Brown.			
25	General Robert C. Buchanan	*Nephew*, Robert Sanford	Poughkeepsie, N. Y.	1879

No. of Names, List I.	Members' Names and Titles.	Blood-relative Elected.		
		Relationship—Names.	Residence.	Date.
26	General George C. Cadwalader	*Nephew*, Dr. C. E. Cadwalader	Philadelphia, Pa.	1886
27	General Albemarle Cady	*Nephew*, N. W. Cady	Logansport, Ia.	1886
28	Colonel G. A. Caldwell.			
29	Lieutenant Robert C. Caldwell.			
30	Colonel George W. Carr.			
31	Colonel Daniel T. Chandler.			
32	General P. St. George Cooke	*Son*, J. R. Cooke	Richmond, Va.	1886
33	Professor Henry Coppée	*Son*, H. St. L. Coppée	Vicksburg, Miss.	1879
34	Colonel Lewis S. Craig.			
35	Surgeon Presly H. Craig	*Nephew*, Isaac Craig	Allegheny City, Pa.	1880
36	Lieutenant Alexander H. Cross	*Nephew*, Jessie L. Reno	Denver, Col.	1886
37	Major Joseph Daniels.			
38	Major J. Y. Dashiell	*Son*, Geo. R. Dashiell.		
39	Colonel George Deas.			
40	Surgeon D. C. DeLeon.			
41	Lieutenant F. J. Denman.			
42	Colonel James Duncan.			
43	General Richard S. Ewell.			
44	General Thomas T. Fauntleroy.			
45	Major Edward H. Fitzgerald.			
46	Colonel Robert C. Forsyth	*Son*, John B. Forsyth	Mobile, Ala.	1886
47	General William H. French	*Son*, Lieutenant Wm. H. French, Jr.	U. S. Army	1879
48	General Daniel M. Frost	*Son*, R. G. Frost	St. Louis, Mo.	1879
49	Major A. W. Gaines.			
50	Colonel Patrick H. Galt.			
51	Colonel John W. T. Gardiner.			
52	General Richard C. Gatlin.			
53	General Alfred Gibbs	*Son*, Alfred W. Gibbs	Richmond, Va.	1886
54	General C. C. Gilbert	*Son*, W. P. Gilbert	Fort Yates, Dakota	1887
55	General Adley H. Gladden.			
56	Major John H. Gore.			
57	Captain Henry D. Grafton	*Nephew*, J. Grafton Minot	Boston, Mass.	1886

	RESIDENT				
58	Gal U. S. Grant, U. S.	Son, Col nel	Gal D.	New Yk cit y, N. Y.	1879
59	Gal John B. Gn	S a, J. B.	agn	New Orl a, La.	1 8 7
60	Gal My Gregg.				
61	Gal tr V. Hagner -	Mg, R dall Hagner		Whin gt, D. C.	1879
62	tin O. P. hin.				
63	Gal Schu vlr hin.				
64	Major Ed l. h.	Son, Ed P.	hd, Jr.	Eton, Md.	1881
65	tin Ed L. F. due	Son, has H. (	die		
66	Gal Hm J.				
67	Surgeon Benjamin F. Hy.				
68	1 fal William S. Hy.				
69	Major John S. Hatheway.	S on, Mk B. Hatch.			
70	Gal aul O. Ht	Son, Paul O.	B	Ma, Ga	1886
71	Mr Hn S. H-	Son, Gly V. Hry		U. S. Army	1886
72	Gal William hin	Gn, I. W. He		Ge f ol Kobbe, U. S. A.	1887
73	An E. B. Hy.				
74	Gal Jph hd.		Hr Hd	Chicago, Ill.	86
75					
76	Major John E. hd.	Nephew, Jph	Jph	Hg, Va.	89
77	Gal Benjamin Huger - Vin.	S on, Eustis Huger			
78	An Is R. Jh.	Nephew, Jph B. Johnston		Hn, D. C.	8i
79	Gal Jph E.	Grandson, L. Ap. R. Jns		Nw York city, N. Y.	86
80	Gl Hn Jones Hy	Son, J hn Hs Hy		Hk, N. J	86
81	Gel Philip Hy				
82	Gel Edmund Hby.				
83	nal C. H. Laub.				
84	Gel George W. Lay.	Son,	Je		
85	Gal Bt E.	Son,	Gal G. W. C.	gin, Va.	1881
86	Gal Mld Lovell.				
87	An Ed A. Hr.				
8	Gal George B. Mlellan.				
89	Major Hp W.	Son, Hn C.	Hn	Me Gt H, S. C.	1886
90	Gal Samuel dd.	Son, Hn W.	Ml	Savannah, Ga	1885
9i	Gal Will in W. Mall				
9i	Major. Jas McKinstry.				
93	An George Ml ne.				

No. of List I.	Members' Names and Titles.	Relationship—Names.	Date Elected. Residence.	Date.
94	General John B. Magruder.			
95	Lieutenant James R. May.			
96	Brevet 1st ... 1st Jul'an May.			
97	Major Albert S. ... Mer.			
98	...el R bert M. ...ris	*Nephew*, M. M. Duncan	Chattanooga, Tenn.	1882
-9-	Colonel Thompson ... Mis	*Son*, J. H. Morris	Litchfield, Minn.	1886
100	Captain F. S. Mumford.			
101	Colonel John Munroe.			
102	General Abraham C. Myers	*Son*, William H. Myers	Washington, D. C.	1881
103	Colonel ...h D. Nelson.			
104	Major Washington I. Newton.			
105	General ...m A. ...ls	*Son*, W. A. Nichols	U. S. Army	1886
106	Colonel Theodore O'Hara.			
1g	Major Francis N. Page	*Son*, F. N. Page	Las Vegas, N. M.	1886
108	...al Innis N. Palmer	*Son*, I. N. Palmer, Jr	Rockdale, Tex.	1883
1g	...al Robert Patterson	*Son*, ...al R. E. ... ...on	Philadelphia, Pa.	879
110	...al John C. Pemberton.			
111	1 ...al Franklin ...re; PRESIDENT U.S.			
112	Major William H. Polk.			
113	1 ...al Andrew Porter	*Son*, J. ...ie P rter	Philadelphia, Pa.	1882
114	General Fitz John Porter	*Son*, H. F. J. Porter	New ...k ...y, N. Y.	1880
115	...al William Preston	*Son*, Robert W. Preston		1879
116	...al John A. Quitman.			
117	Major ...ge W. Rains.			
118	Surgeon Burton Randall	*Son*, Alexander B. Randall	...olis, Md.	1886
1g	General Jesse L. Reno ... ...t.	*Son*, Conrad Reno	Boston, Mass.	1886
120	...el ...las G. ...t.			
121	Surgeon Robert R. ...ie.			
122	General Roswell S. Ripley.			
123	Brevet 1st Lieut. F. S. K. Russell.			

Page 16	General Winfield Scott *	Grandson, Winfield Scott Hoyt	New York city, N. Y.	1887
124	Colonel Henry L. Scott	Son, Winfield Scott	New York city, N. Y.	1879
125	General Oliver L. Shepherd	Son, John M. Shepherd	New York city, N. Y.	1880
126	Captain Hamilton L. Shields.			
127	General Henry H. Sibley.			
128	Colonel James Simons	Grandson, G. L. Dulany	Baltimore, Md.	1886
129	General Charles F. Smith	Son, Captain Allen Smith	U. S. Army	1886
130	General Gustavus W. Smith.			
131	General Martin L. Smith.	Son, Victor Smith	Baltimore, Md.	1879
132	General P. F. Smith.			
133	General William Steele.			
134	Colonel Edward J. Steptoe.			
135	Colonel Adam D. Steuart.			
136	General Charles P. Stone.	Son, John Stone, *nominated*	New York city, N. Y.	1886
137	Captain James Stuart.			
138	General George Sykes	Son, Macrae Sykes	New York city, N. Y.	1886
139	Captain Francis J. Thomas.			
140	Major Philip R. Thompson.			
141	Captain Herman Thorn.			
142	Lieutenant James Tilton.			
143	General John B. S. Todd.			
144	General Zealous B. Tower.	*Nephew,* Benjamin M. Tower	Boston, Mass.	1879
145	Surgeon Chas. S. Tripler.			
146	Colonel William Turnbull	Son, William Turnbull	New York city, N. Y.	1883
147	Colonel D. E. Twiggs	Son, John W. Twiggs	San Francisco, Cal.	1886
148	Colonel Abraham Van Buren	Son, Travis C. Van Buren	New York city, N. Y.	1886
149	General Earl Van Dorn.			
150	Colonel Richard D. A. Wade.			
151	General Cadmus M. Wilcox.			
152	Colonel John D. Wilkins.			
153	General Thomas Williams	Son, John R. Williams	U. S. Army	1886
154	General John S. Williams.			
155	General Jones M. Withers.			
156	Major George W. F. Wood.			
157	Captain Lafayette B. Wood.			
158	Major Francis Woodbridge	Son, Francis Woodbridge	U. S. Army	1882

* Honorary Member—Page 16, List I.

CPSIA information can be obtained
at www.ICGtesting.com
Printed in the USA
BVHW091239261118
534010BV00012B/229/P